Inside My Body

How Do My Braces Work?

Steve Parker

Raintree

Chicago, Illinois

Edited by Kate de Villiers and Laura Knowles
Designed by Steve Mead
Illustrations by KJA-artists.com
Picture research by Mica Brancic

Originated by Capstone Global Library Ltd
Printed in the United States of America by Worzalla
Publishing

15 14 13 12 11 10
10 9 8 7 6 5 4 3 2 1

Library of Congress Cataloging-in-Publication Data
Parker, Steve, 1952-
   How do braces work? : teeth / Steve Parker.
      p. cm. — (Inside my body)
   Includes bibliographical references and index.
   ISBN 978-1-4109-4019-3 — ISBN 978-1-4109-4030-
8 1. Teeth—Juvenile literature. 2. Teeth—Care and
hygiene—Juvenile literature. 3. Orthodontic appliances—
Juvenile literature. I. Title. II. Title: Teeth.
   QP88.6.P37 2011
   612.3'11—dc22   2010024805

Acknowledgments
The author and publisher are grateful to the following
for permission to reproduce copyright material: Alamy
p. **13** (© Pixel Shepherd); iStockphoto pp. **24** (© Jozsef
Szasz-Fabian), **15** (© Kirk Strickland); Photolibrary pp. **6**
(age fotostock/Gustavo Andrade), **21** (Corbis), **4** (Design
Pics Inc), **7** (Design Pics Inc/Chris Knorr), **16** (Digital
Light Source/Richard Hutchings), **10** (Flirt Collection/
Jim Cornfield), **5** (Imagestate RM/Michael L. Peck),
18 (Moodboard RF), **8** (Radius Images), **17** (Somos
Images/Bill Varie); Science Photo Library p. **20** (Tirot);
Shutterstock pp. **14** (Adrian Hughes), **25** (Paul Prescott),
27 (© Monkey Business Images), **19** (© Ragne Kabanova).

Photographic design details reproduced with permission
of Shutterstock pp. **7**, **9**, **13**, **15**, **16**, **21**, **22** (© Isaac
Marzioli), **7**, **9**, **13**, **15**, **16**, **21**, **22** (© Yurok).

Cover photograph of girl with braces reproduced
with permission of Getty Images/Brand X Pictures/
Andersen Ross.

We would like to thank David Wright for his invaluable
help in the preparation of this book.

Every effort has been made to contact copyright holders
of any material reproduced in this book. Any omissions
will be rectified in subsequent printings if notice is given
to the publisher.

All the Internet addresses (URLs) given in this book were
valid at the time of going to press. However, due to the
dynamic nature of the Internet, some addresses may
have changed, or sites may have changed or ceased to
exist since publication. While the author and publisher
regret any inconvenience this may cause readers, no
responsibility for any such changes can be accepted by
either the author or the publisher.

Contents

Words that appear in the text in bold, **like this**, are explained in the glossary on page 30.

Why Do Some People Wear Braces?

Do you wear braces on your teeth, or do you know someone who does? Some children wear braces to help their teeth grow straight, without gaps or crowding that could cause problems when they grow up. A few adults wear braces, too.

Why are teeth important?

There are many reasons why teeth are so important:

- You use them to bite and chew food before swallowing. This stops you from choking on big pieces of food.
- Chewing also helps your body to digest the food well and get the most **nutrients** from it.
- You need teeth to speak properly. Try saying "the" without your tongue touching your teeth.

🔎 If you are lucky, you will be able to choose what color your braces are.

Lots of teeth

An adult has 32 teeth. This may seem like a lot, but some animals have many more. For example, some dolphins have as many as 250 teeth.

A tiger has 30 teeth. They include four very long, pointed ones called canines.

What Do My Teeth Look Like?

How much do you know about your teeth? Keeping an eye on your teeth helps you to take good care of them and notice any problems.

Two sets of teeth

The human body has two sets of teeth. First is the baby set of 20 teeth. These gradually fall out naturally from about the age of six. They are replaced by the adult set of 32 teeth.

Each tooth is shaped for a particular job. Your front teeth are slim and sharp to bite through food. Toward the back of your mouth, your teeth are wider and blunter, for powerful chewing.

🔍 **Give your teeth a good check every few days.**

Tooth check

Look closely at your teeth every few days. Use a bright light above, such as the light over a bathroom mirror, or a flashlight. Open your mouth wide and use your fingers to pull back your lips and cheeks.

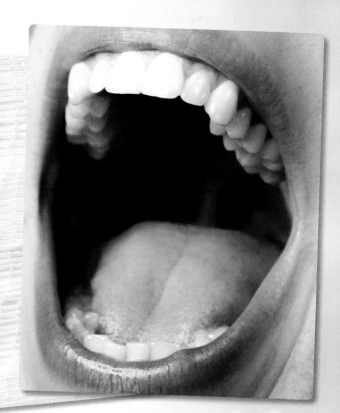

Anything odd?

Look for anything unusual in your teeth. Maybe you have some new adult teeth growing, which are still quite small. Perhaps a tooth has a white patch or a wavy edge. Mention it at your next visit to the dentist. The dentist will probably say that all is well.

SCIENCE BEHIND THE MYTH

MYTH: White teeth are the strongest.

SCIENCE: Not always. Slightly yellow teeth can be strong and healthy. But very yellow or very gray teeth should be checked by a dentist.

What Do My Teeth Do?

The main jobs for teeth are to bite off pieces of food and chew the pieces so they are soft and ready to swallow.

Biting

You can fit small food items such as peas or rice into your mouth. But you cannot fit a whole melon or a complete cooked chicken! Your front teeth, called incisors, have sharp edges, like tiny blades. These slice or nibble big foods and cut off small pieces to fit into your mouth.

🔍 **Incisor teeth at the front of the mouth have sharp edges that easily cut through softer foods.**

Next to your incisors are your canine teeth, also called cuspids. These are slightly longer and more pointed. They are good for tearing and pulling bits off foods that are difficult to bite all the way through.

Chewing

Your back teeth are called **premolars** and molars. Their wide, flat tops are ideal for chewing food into a soft mush for easy swallowing. As you chew food, you mix it with saliva (spit). This makes the lumps soft and slippery for swallowing. Saliva also helps to wash bits of old food off your teeth. It contains substances that protect teeth and substances that start the breakdown of food.

Practical advice

Why chewing is good

Try to chew every mouthful of food at least 30 times.

- Chewing helps to break up the food, so you get more **nutrients**.
- It prevents you from choking if you try to swallow big, hard pieces of food.
- It helps to exercise your jaws and jaw muscles.
- It gives you time to taste delicious foods properly.

Why Do Baby Teeth Fall Out?

You have only two sets of teeth during your life. There are 20 teeth in the first set, called infant, baby, or **primary teeth**. Some babies have a few teeth when they are born, but most have none. Baby teeth usually start to appear from the age of six months, and they are all grown by the age of three.

Once baby teeth have appeared, they cannot grow any larger. However, the jaws and the rest of the body do grow bigger. If the baby teeth stayed until adulthood, they would be too small and weak for the size of the mouth and jaws. This is why the body develops a second, bigger set of teeth.

🔍 **The first baby teeth to appear are the lower incisors at the front, followed by the upper incisors above them.**

Adult teeth

When a child is about six years old, baby teeth start to fall out. The adult or **permanent teeth** start to appear. Usually they finish growing by the time a person is 20 years old. No more teeth will ever grow, so it is important to take good care of them.

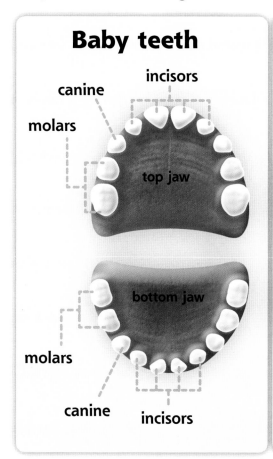

Baby teeth

canine
incisors
molars
top jaw
bottom jaw
molars
canine
incisors

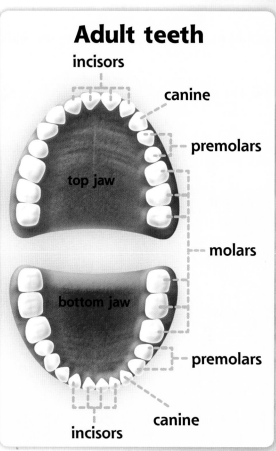

Adult teeth

incisors
canine
premolars
top jaw
molars
bottom jaw
premolars
canine
incisors

SCIENCE BEHIND THE MYTH

MYTH: Wisdom teeth make you wise.

SCIENCE: Not really. The four molar teeth at the very back of the mouth are called "wisdom teeth" because they only appear in adults, who are supposed to be wise. But not all adults have them. On average, about one person in five never grows wisdom teeth. Usually, this is because the person's mouth is too small.

What's Inside a Tooth?

The upper part of a tooth, which you can see above the gum, is known as the **crown**. The lower part, which you cannot see, is fixed firmly into the jawbone. This part is called the **root**.

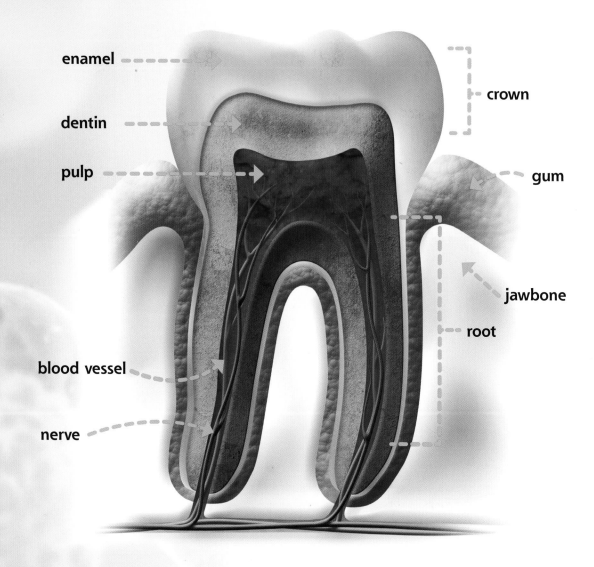

enamel

dentin

pulp

crown

gum

jawbone

root

blood vessel

nerve

This diagram shows the inside of a molar tooth.

On the outside

The outside layer of the crown is made of **enamel**. This is the hardest substance in the body, because it has to bite and chew for years without wearing away. Under the enamel is another layer, almost as hard, called **dentin**. This is more like bone and can be crushed very slightly. It helps to absorb some of the pressure as you munch and crunch hard foods.

On the inside

In the middle of a tooth is the soft **dental pulp**. This has tiny **blood vessels** that bring **nutrients** to keep the whole tooth alive and healthy. Pulp also has tiny nerves to feel problems such as too much pressure on the tooth, or a toothache.

Practical advice

Broken tooth

If you break a tooth, get to the dentist quickly. If you can find the broken-off part, put it in a clean plastic bag and take it with you. The dentist will stop the tooth from becoming **infected** and start to fix it as much as possible.

What's Bad for My Teeth?

Many people like candy, cookies, cakes, chocolates, and soft drinks. But too much of these foods can be bad for the body—especially the teeth.

Dentists often use a small mirror to help them see inside a patient's mouth.

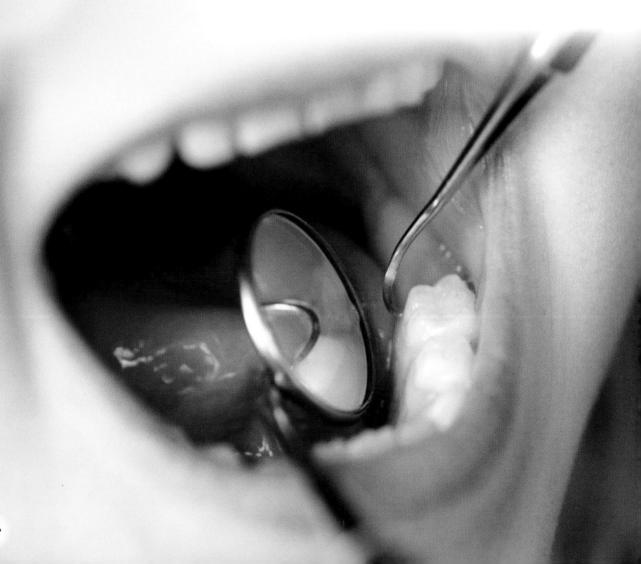

Sugar and acid

Sweet foods have lots of sugar in them. The problem is that sugar is also food for **bacteria**. These live on and in our bodies all the time. They usually cause no harm. However, if you eat too many sugary foods, the bacteria in your mouth feed on the sugar and produce a waste substance—acid. This acid can damage your teeth. It weakens the **enamel** and even makes holes in it. This is known as tooth decay.

Plaque

If teeth are not cleaned, old pieces of food, dead bacteria, their waste, and other yucky stuff collect as a thin layer called **dental plaque**. If this is still not cleaned, it can build into thicker lumps that do great harm to the teeth and gums.

Practical advice

Protect teeth

Some high-speed sports can damage teeth. If you play them, make sure that you wear the best protection, such as a mouthguard and helmet.

Why Do I Clean My Teeth?

There are many reasons to clean your teeth—to keep them and your gums healthy, to make your mouth feel fresh and clean, and to avoid the smell of bad breath.

Practical advice

When to clean teeth

The best times to clean teeth are after meals and at bedtime. After a meal, bacteria feed on small pieces of food left in your mouth, making acid that damages tooth enamel. Cleaning your teeth at bedtime means bacteria cannot spend all night causing damage.

How to clean teeth

The three main ways to clean teeth are brushing, flossing, and using mouthwash. Your dentist or another expert, the **dental hygienist**, can show you how. Brush every tooth on both sides, on its top, around its base with the gum, and between it and the next tooth.

Brushing also cleans food and **bacteria** off your gums. Otherwise the gums become swollen, red, and painful, and they may bleed. This type of gum disease is known as gingivitis.

Fluoride

To brush well, you need a strong toothbrush and a toothpaste containing fluoride. The substance fluoride makes **enamel** stronger, so tooth decay is less likely. In many places, tiny amounts of fluoride are added to drinking water, to help everyone's teeth.

The dentist or hygienist can show you how to floss without harming your teeth or gums.

Why Do I Go to the Dentist?

The dentist checks your teeth to see that you are taking good care of them and that they are healthy, well-spaced, straight, and growing properly. The dentist also looks at the gums around the teeth to make sure they are healthy, too.

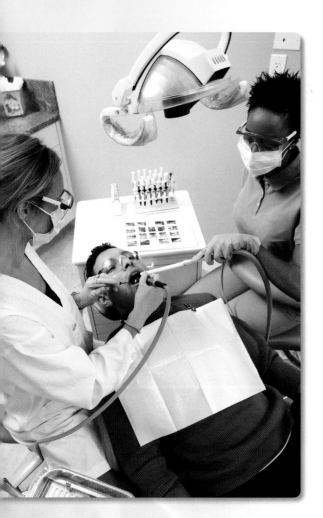

Open wide!

Most people go to the dentist every six months or each year. The dentist looks at each tooth in detail. A gurgling tube in your mouth sucks away saliva, to give the dentist a clear view. He or she pokes and taps the teeth and gums to make sure they are not painful. For each visit, the dentist makes a record of the health of every tooth and of your gums.

🔍 **The dentist and dental hygienist use many tools and gadgets to help your teeth and gums stay healthy.**

The dentist may show you how to brush and floss your teeth and use a mouthwash. The **dental hygienist** shows you how to keep your whole mouth clean and healthy.

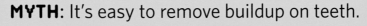

SCIENCE BEHIND THE MYTH

MYTH: It's easy to remove buildup on teeth.

SCIENCE: No, it's not! Sometimes a tough substance called calculus or tartar builds up on teeth, and it is like a harder version of **dental plaque**. It cannot be removed by ordinary tooth brushing. The dentist has to clean teeth, usually with a tiny, powerful jet of water.

X-rays can "see" inside parts of the body. Dentists take an X-ray of the mouth so they can see any tiny cracks or holes in the teeth, the health of the gums and tooth **roots**, and any teeth still in the jawbone.

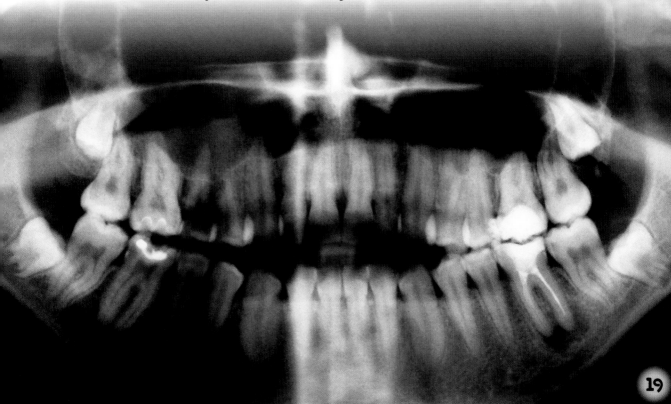

How Do Braces Work?

Braces help teeth to grow straight, look good, and stay healthy. They can also make biting and chewing more comfortable. They are fitted by the dentist or another tooth expert, the **orthodontist**.

Made to measure

Most types of braces press on the teeth gently over a long period. This slowly pushes the teeth as they grow, to make them straighter and fit together properly. Braces are made to measure, to fit just one person. The dentist or orthodontist checks and adjusts them regularly.

🔍 **This child is having braces fitted onto her teeth.**

SCIENCE BEHIND THE MYTH ?

MYTH: Braces always hurt.

SCIENCE: If braces are fitted properly, and the wearer gets used to them, they should not hurt. If they do, they may have been pushed out of shape. The wearer should go back to the dentist.

Types of braces

Fixed braces stay in the mouth for long periods, perhaps months. Removable braces and retainers can be taken out for cleaning or on special occasions. Head gears have a frame that fits around the head and are usually worn at night.

Sometimes teeth are too crowded. The dentist may take out one or two and use braces to move the other teeth along to fill the gap.

Practical advice

Tooth cleaning for braces or retainers

When wearing braces or retainers, tooth cleaning is very important. Cutting down on sticky or sugary foods and drinks is essential. The dentist may suggest a special fluoride cream or a germ-killing mouthwash.

What's a Toothache?

If people do not keep their teeth and gums healthy, sooner or later they will get a toothache. This is one of the worst kinds of pain. It can hurt terribly until a dentist treats it.

Eating away teeth

As **bacteria** feed on old food in the mouth, they produce acids that eat into the tooth **enamel**, making it soft and weak. This is tooth decay. If the tooth is not fixed, eventually a hole or cavity appears. Fluid from the mouth leaks into the tooth's **dental pulp** and affects the nerves there, causing a toothache.

Practical advice

Help for a toothache

If you have a toothache but cannot see the dentist right away, there are several things you can do:

- Use a dental mouthwash or a mouth rinse of warm, slightly salty water.
- Use a special cream from a pharmacy on your gums to ease the pain.
- Avoid hard, crunchy foods.

Tooth abscess

Sometimes germs get into the pulp inside the tooth, making it start to swell and hurt. This **infection** can spread down the **root** into the jawbone, producing a horrible-tasting liquid called pus. This may form a painful swelling known as an abscess.

SCIENCE BEHIND THE MYTH

MYTH: A toothache can get better on its own.

SCIENCE: This is not true. A sprained wrist or a cut finger usually gets better. But left alone, a toothache almost always gets worse. The only cure is a trip to the dentist.

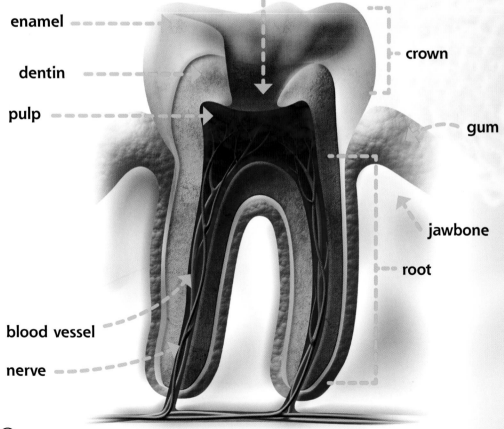

tooth decay (cavity caused by bacteria)

enamel

dentin

pulp

crown

gum

jawbone

root

blood vessel

nerve

If not treated, tooth decay can eat away enamel and **dentin** and get into the soft, sensitive pulp.

How Are Teeth Fixed?

If tooth decay is just beginning, the dentist may be able to treat it by painting a special liquid onto the tooth. If the decay is deeper, the usual way to fix it is to put in a filling.

Drill and fill

To repair a decayed tooth, the dentist first gives the patient an injection to prevent pain. Then the decayed part of the tooth is quickly drilled away to make a clean hole. Into this is put a very hard substance, the filling. Some fillings are made from several substances, mixed to be the same color as the tooth. Other fillings are made of metal and are a silvery color. Another choice is a gold metal filling.

🔍 **Metal fillings are usually a silvery substance called amalgam.**

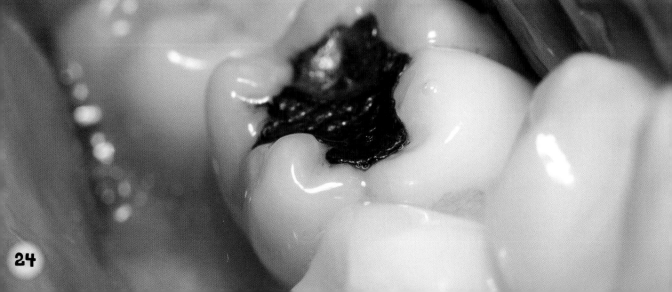

Taken out

If the decay is quite bad, the dentist may remove most of the tooth's upper part and put on a false top, called a dental **crown**. With really bad decay, the whole tooth may have to be taken out. A false tooth, made of very hard plastic or metal, can be put in its place.

SCIENCE BEHIND THE MYTH

MYTH: False teeth soon wear away.

SCIENCE: Some people think that false teeth, called **dentures**, are weak and soon wear away. But modern false teeth are extremely strong and tough. A whole false tooth, including the **root**, is called a tooth implant. Modern tooth implants made from the metal titanium are almost as hard as a real tooth.

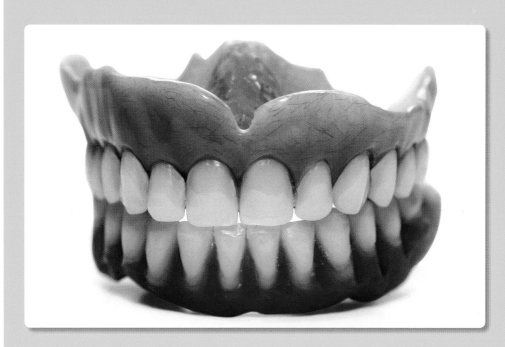

How Can I Take Care of My Teeth?

If your teeth are not healthy, they soon let you know. You might get a toothache and have trouble eating and talking. You only have one set of adult teeth, so take good care of them!

Happy teeth checklist

Remember the main ways to care for your teeth:

- Do not eat too many sweet or sugary foods.
- Avoid snacks and sweets between meals.
- Clean teeth at least twice a day—after breakfast and before bed. If possible, clean them after every meal.
- Brush your teeth with a fluoride toothpaste, and use floss and mouthwash if the dentist says these are right for you.
- Visit the dentist once or twice each year for a full checkup.
- If you get a toothache, or break a tooth in an accident, see the dentist as soon as possible.
- Keep smiling!

SCIENCE BEHIND THE MYTH

MYTH: Some foods clean your teeth.

SCIENCE: This is not true. Some people say that if you eat certain foods, such as apples, you do not have to clean your teeth afterward. But any food can leave bits in the mouth for the **bacteria** to eat. However, eating does make saliva come into the mouth, which helps to protect teeth. A dry mouth is bad for teeth.

Thorough cleaning and help from braces will make teeth look good and last a lifetime.

The Body's Two Sets of Teeth

Everyone's teeth are different in size, shape, and color. They grow and fall out at different times. But most people have teeth like those shown here. Look in the mirror and compare your own teeth to the pictures on this page.

Baby teeth and when they appear

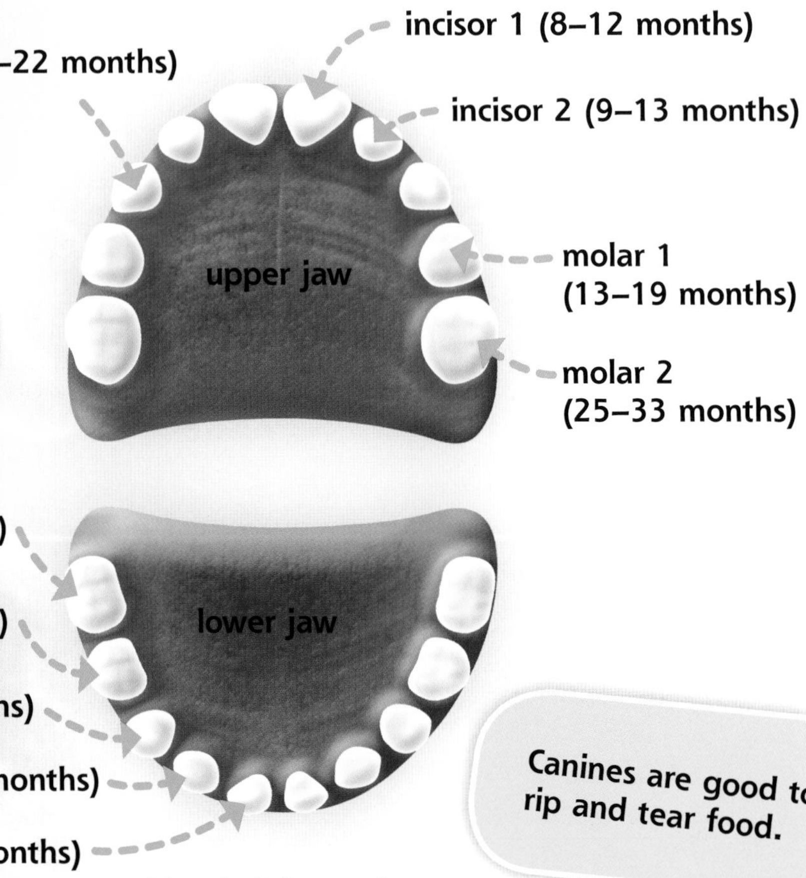

canine (16–22 months)

incisor 1 (8–12 months)

incisor 2 (9–13 months)

Molars are known as "cheek teeth" because they are on the insides of the cheeks.

upper jaw

molar 1 (13–19 months)

molar 2 (25–33 months)

molar 2 (23–31 months)

molar 1 (14–18 months)

lower jaw

canine (17–23 months)

incisor 2 (10–16 months)

incisor 1 (6–10 months)

Canines are good to rip and tear food.

Total: 20 teeth

Incisors are best for biting, slicing, and nibbling.

Premolars chew and crush foods.

Adult teeth and when they appear

canine (11–12 years)

incisor 1 (7–8 years)

incisor 2 (8–9 years)

The canine is sometimes called the "eye tooth" because it is directly below the eye.

upper jaw

premolar 1 (10–11 years)

premolar 2 (10–12 years)

molar 1 (6–7 years)

molar 2 (12–13 years)

molar 3 (17–21 years)

lower jaw

molar 3 (17–21 years)

molar 2 (11–13 years)

molar 1 (6–7 years)

premolar 2 (11–12 years)

premolar 1 (10–11 years)

canine (9–10 years)

incisor 2 (7–8 years)

incisor 1 (6–7 years)

The four molar 3 teeth, at the back of each side of the jaw, are the "wisdom teeth." You may only grow these if your mouth is big enough. In some people, they never appear, but they might be under the gums.

Total: 32 teeth

Molars are most powerful for crushing and crunching.

Glossary

bacteria tiny living things that are too small to see except under a microscope. Some types cause infection and disease.

blood vessel pipe-like tube that carries blood around the body

crown upper part of a tooth that is covered with enamel and shows above the gum

dental hygienist expert at keeping teeth, gums, and the whole mouth clean and healthy

dental plaque gooey mixture of old food, living and dead bacteria, and acid that can build up on teeth

dental pulp soft inner part of a tooth, with nerves and blood vessels

dentin hard middle layer of a tooth, between the enamel and the pulp

dentures false teeth on a removable plate that fits onto the gums

enamel extremely hard outer layer of a tooth

infection when germs get into a body part and cause disease

nutrient substance needed by the body for energy and to grow and repair itself

orthodontist specialist in treating crooked or crowded teeth, teeth with gaps, and other similar problems

permanent teeth adult teeth; the body's second and last set of teeth

premolars fairly wide, flat-topped teeth toward the rear of the mouth, between the canines and the molars

primary teeth baby teeth; the body's first set of teeth

root in a tooth, the lower part of the tooth that fixes it in the jawbone below the gum

Find Out More

Books

Collard, Sneed B., and Phyllis V Saroff. *Teeth.* New York: Scholastic, 2008.

Llewellyn, Claire. *Your Teeth* (*Looking After Yourself*). Mankato, Minn.: Sea-to-Sea, 2008.

Miller, Edward. *The Tooth Book: A Guide to Healthy Teeth and Gums.* New York: Scholastic, 2009.

Websites

http://kidshealth.org/kid/htbw/teeth.html

You can read several information-packed articles about teeth on this website.

www.adha.org/kidstuff/index.html

Visit this website about teeth, which offers games, answers to common questions, and some quick facts.

www.mouthpower.org/mouthpower.cfm

This fun website has lots of games and activities about teeth.

Index